A Collection of Poetic Gems

Valerie Dawson

Copyright © 2019 Valerie Dawson

Book design by Power of Words.
Cover image: Pixabay/sandid

All rights reserved. No part of this book may be reproduced in any form by any electronic or mechanical means including photocopying, recording, or information storage and retrieval without permission in writing from the author.

ISBN-13: 978-0-9945105-3-2

 A catalogue record for this book is available from the National Library of Australia

www.powerofwords.com.au/books

Published by Power of Words, Clontarf, QLD.
Printed in Australia.
Please give feedback on the book wherever it was bought.

Dedication

In memory of my darling late husband, Donald.
Always in our thoughts.

Table of Contents

Author's Note 1
Praise to Australia 3
Australia Wins The America's Cup 5
Sail with the Navy 7
"The Nashos" 8
Much Ado at Mt. Mellum 9
A Horse Named MO 12

Places Close to my Heart: London, England 15
Come to London with Me (no. 2) 16
Come to London with Me (no. 3) 17
Happy Diamond Jubilee 18

Interesting People 19
A Man called Hawke 20
A Tribute to Ron Grant 21

Places Close to my Heart: Queensland 25
Bountiful Queensland 26
Most Bountiful Queensland (no. 1) 27
Most Bountiful Queensland (no. 2) 28
Brisbane: My Favourite Place 29
Heritage Ipswich City 30
Ipswich. The Heritage City 31
Ode to Brisbane 33
Sydney on the Harbour 34
Redcliffe by the Sea 35

Mighty Mares	37
Our Star – Black Caviar	38
One-in-a-Million Winx	40
The Sydney Olympics are Here	44
Gold Coast Commonwealth Games are Here	45
ODE to the Broncos	46
ODE to the MAROONS	47
Ode to the West Coast Eagles	48
Poems for Children	49
Welcome K.C. the Cat	50
In Memory of Laleh	51
Happy Australia Day	53
Making Easter Eggs	55
The Xmas Bilbies	56
You're Never Too Old for Santa Claus	57

Author's Note

I like to write poems about places, events, people and animals. I have loved poetry since I was at school. My style of writing would be called "imagery". For some poems, I would be inspired to adapt them a little and compose music for them.

The first poem I did this with was about the yacht race for The America's Cup. I called the song, "The America's Cup Waltz" and I even made up a dance to go with it. I sent a copy of the recording over to Prince Phillip, and I received a letter of thanks in reply from his secretary to say how much the Queen and Duke had enjoyed it. (I wonder if they also did the dance, as I enclosed instructions!)

I only wrote poetry and composed lyrics and music as a hobby, mostly after I retired. The first poem that I composed and is published here, was in 1965, as I was too busy raising a family and working. The poems and CD of my songs are in the National Archives in Canberra. *A Collection of Musical Gems* is the name of my CD.

NB. *Imagist:* A poet who uses ordinary speech and precise presentation, in a style called Imagery.

Valerie Dawson

A Collection of Poetic Gems

Praise to Australia

Once upon a dreamtime,
Land and Nature were as one,
to Aboriginal Tribes this was home.

Now they've shared it with us,
The wealth, the beauty so sublime,
Who'll give their all, from
These shores never roam.

Praise to Australia, our home Australia,
Who'll do their best to help keep this land free,
And rejoice as we go, about our daily work or play,
So proud, that we live in this great country.

Here today are people every creed and every race.
Let's pull as one, for harmony and grace.
Build a mighty Nation
A land of peace and liberty
For new generations, for you and me.

Praise to Australia, our home Australia,
Who'll do their best to help keep this land free,
And rejoice as we go about our daily work or play.

So proud, that we live in this great country.
So proud that we live in this great country.

© 1996 – 2010. Valerie Dawson
Music to the tune of "Waltzing Matilda" (by Maree Cowan).
YouTube: http://bit.ly/PraisetoOz

Valerie Dawson

Australia Wins 'The America's Cup'

Oh! I am The America's Cup, they call me ugly but won't give me up.
Oh! I am The America's Cup, for too many years I've been bolted up. For too many years, I've been bolted up.

For over a century, many nations have tried,
To win me for glory, for tourists and pride.
Bond, Bertram and Lexcen and all the yacht crew,
You came with gold spanner, my bolt to unscrew.
Now Australia 2 has won me,
With a new kind of keel,
Which to the world watching, all seems unreal.

Imprisoned in a glass case for so many years,
I'm leaving the Americans midst eyes full of tears.
For a brief time I touched down on ancestral soil,
Maybe one day "Victory" will have me as spoil.
And now that I've landed in Perth, I'll be dutiful,
And who knows, the swans there may think that I'm beautiful.

Three years have soon passed, and the challenge draws nigh,
Freemantle is hosting Yacht Clubs that will vie.
Britons, Kiwis and Americans, just to mention a few,
You're here with yachts, mainsails and spinnakers' bright hues.
Though the currents are quite tricky, and on this West Coast unknown,
The Americans have won me and taken me home.

Valerie Dawson

Now Morcom sent out a challenge from Mercury Bay,
To wrest me from Connors, came good Michael Fay.
A thirty-eight metre yacht, with sixteen-storey high sails,
'Gainst a catamaran, one must surely fail.
But the courts ruled the match foul,
San Diego must give, the Cup to New Zealand, at Whitianga I'll live.

Oh! I am the America's Cup, they call me ugly but won't give me up.
Oh! I am the America's Cup, for too many years
I've been bolted up; for too many years I've been bolted up.

© 1983 Music and vocals: Valerie Dawson. Played D. Cobbin.
'Victory' was a British yacht in an America's Cup race.
Adapted for a recording. Record and poem in Maritime Museum, Fremantle.
YouTube: http://bit.ly/AustwinsAmericasCup

SAIL WITH THE NAVY

Our young naval men, and women too,
Australia's so proud of you,
Not khaki, not blue, but navy,
Come aboard, be part of the crew

Serving your country at peace or at war,
Protecting your homeland, patrolling its shore,
With the Navy, the Navy, the Senior Service, the Navy
You'll sail the ocean blue, sail the ocean blue,
You'll sail on the ocean blue so wavy

For a brilliant career, the Navy's the place,
On a frigate or Sub, every sailor's an ace,
With all this great training, your future's assured,
You'll visit new places, you'll travel abroad
With the Navy, the Navy, the Royal Australian Navy.

So come on, be brave, it's anchors away,
And sail the ocean blue, sail the ocean blue,
And sail on the ocean blue so wavy

© 2008 Valerie Dawson.
CD made. Music/vocals V. Dawson. Played & arranged D. Cobbin.
Played in concert by R.A.N. Band on H.M.A.S. Cerberus Melbourne.
YouTube: http://bit.ly/SailNavy

Valerie Dawson

"The Nashos"

The National Servicemen of Australia,
They were willing, they were raw, they were young,
The National Servicemen of Australia,
Had to learn how to handle a gun.

They served in the Navy, the Army and the Air Force,
Where their lives quickly took a new course,
In the Navy, the Army and the Air Force,
They were willing, they were raw, they were young,

They had to be ready, in the event of a war,
Or in case foreign countries invaded our shore,
The National Servicemen of Australia,
They were willing, they were raw, they were young,

They had to leave their families,
   their sweethearts and their mates,
Their names were called if they were born
    within those certain dates
They had to do route marches, toting heavy packs,
With blistered feet and aching limbs,
    they longed to hit their sacks.

But they did many years of tough training,
With hardly a thought of complaining,
They came out strong, they came out fit,
They came out very proud to be,
The National Servicemen of Australia
Let's cheer them long and loud.

© 2000. Composed to commemorate 50 years. Played in concert by Australian Army band. Music and vocals: V. Dawson. Played by: D. Cobbin

MUCH ADO AT MT. MELLUM

At Mt. Mellum there was much ado, for the talk had got around,
That Merv Baderick had a crop of tomatoes, he hoped would fetch five hundred pounds.

So he enquired if neighbour Don Dawson, would do the spraying and weeding,
But alas, all Don's cows, pigs, chooks and calves, needed too much care and feeding.
Don's Missus was asked if she'd like to earn, a bit of extra cash,
But she replied, that picking tomatoes was inclined to give her a rash.

Next he implored Ralph the milkman, to bring him some packing cases,
But Ralph said, "I can't even find the time, to tie up me own boot laces".
Mick Foster, ex cop and Groundsel Inspector, was invited to boil the billy,
But he declined, saying, "Cripes no, Merv, your farm is far too hilly".
Then in desperation, Merv went down, to nearby Landsborough town,
Where he hired the whole Binstead family, who were just lazing around.

Roderick, a cutter of timber and cordwood, thought the pickers all looked wrecks,

Valerie Dawson

When he dropped by to enquire, as to whether Merv had any "specks".
After all the picking and packing, and much banging on of lid,
Merv was convinced, there must be, an easier way to make a quid.

© 1965 Val Dawson

MUCH ADO AT MT MELLUM — FOOTNOTE:

A poem based on an actual event and characters

In 1964, my husband Don and I purchased a dairy and crop farm. It was at Mt Mellum, which is one of the lesser known Glass House mountains, an extinct volcano, about three miles up the Maleny Range from Landsborough. We moved there with our four children and settled into farming life with milking cows, growing many different crops like peas, beans, corn and tomatoes, as well as rearing pigs, calves and poultry and selling eggs.

The area in years previous had been soldier settlement farms, where bananas were grown after WW1. During that time a one-teacher school was on the track leading down to Landsborough. Only the well of the old school remained, which was now on our property.

Our farm had glorious views of the ocean, Caloundra and the other Glasshouse Mountains. Part of our farm extended down to Landsborough. High on the farm was a wonderful spring, (that never ran dry); it was the start of Mellum Creek.

The farm was about 680 acres in size, consisting of grazing land and bush and 50 acres of good crop land. We paid 6,500 pounds for the farm, but today it would be worth many millions of dollars.

We soon got to know our near neighbours and many others on the farms elsewhere on the Maleny Range. Our lives were very busy and eventful.

Valerie Dawson

A Horse Named MO

Come round the fire and gather near,
If you really want to hear.
This story I wrote so long ago.
It's about a great old drover,
Who had a Kelpie dog named Rover,
And a horse with the name of MO.

They experienced floods,
They experienced droughts.
But never once was their friendship in doubt,
They stuck together through thick and through thin.
Mo pulled him out of many a fix,
Mainly using the horse's tail trick.
A greater love there never had been.

Droving along miles of outback track,
Poor Mo had many a saddle-sore back,
But never once did they complain.
They enjoyed each other's company.
Sleeping near a camp fire, happy and free,
And keeping each other sane.

They worked together like this for years,
Never once causing each other tears.
Till one day a brown snake bit MO on the leg.
The drover nursed him night and day,
But alas his true friend he couldn't save.

It was futile, it was useless,
The horse was dead.

He buried MO 'neath a shady tree,
And because near him he wanted to be,
The drover built himself an old slab hut.
Now he spends his days in a rocking chair,
With his old dog and MO's bridle there,
And he thinks of the time when they worked as a team,
   MO, himself, and his faithful Kelpie mutt.

(c) 2007 Valerie Dawson

Valerie Dawson

Places Close to my Heart: London, England

Image: Freepik

Valerie Dawson

Come to London with Me (no. 2)

Come on, come with me to London City,
The City where we'll see it all.
It's Jubilee Year in London City,
Come with me, so we can have a ball.

To the Games we will go, where there'll be the best,
Athletes from around the world put to the test.
So just come with me, and we'll see all the rest.

Trafalgar Square decorated in finest array,
Palace, Tower Bridge, Big Ben, We'll see all in a day.
Down the Thames, we will take a ride on a barge.
And if we're in luck, we might see,
The "Changing of the Guard".

Come on, come with me to London City,
The City where we'll see it all.
It's Jubilee Year in London City,
Come with me so we can have a ball.

Come on, with me, please don't let me down,
So together we can see the Games, the Games in London Town,
Then we'll take in London's every sight and sound.

© 2012
Lyrics, music and vocals by V. Dawson
Music arranged and played by D. Cobbins

COME TO LONDON WITH ME (NO. 3)

Come on, come with me to London City,
The City where we'll see it all.
Come on come with me to London City,
Come with me so we can have a ball.

London Eye we will ride,
Where we'll have a view,
Of this famous City, the old and the new.
So just come with me, you can enjoy it too.

Trafalgar Square, Nelson's Column
With Nelson on top.
Tower Bridge, Big Ben, Palace,
Will be our next stop.
Down the Thames we will take,
Take a ride on a barge.
And if we're in luck, we might see,
The "Changing of the Guard".

So come on with me, to London City.
Let's go for a stroll down Pall Mall.
Come on come with me to London City,
Come and we might see the Royals as well.

Come on with me, please don't let me down,
So together we can see the lights,
The lights of London Town.
Then we'll take in London's every sight and sound.

Lyrics, music and vocals: V. J. Dawson. Music by D. Cobbins.

Valerie Dawson

Happy Diamond Jubilee

Happy Diamond Jubilee
To our Queen across the seas,
With great health and good cheer,
May you reign for many more years.
Happy Diamond Jubilee
Happy Diamond Jubilee.

© 2012. Adapted from "Happy Anniversary".
CD of song sent to the Queen.
Lyrics, music and vocals by V. Dawson
Music arranged and played by D. Cobbins

Interesting People

Valerie Dawson

A Man called Hawke

Who is this man, nicknamed so grand?
He might make this country into the promised land.
A man of strong will, energy and grit,
A diplomat so gracious, he is a world-wide hit.

Rivers now are flowing, right across the land,
Since he came to office, since he made his stand.
Arid wastes are blooming, that only once were sands.
Since he came to power, since he took command.

Bounteous crops are growing in soil
   drought winds once fanned,
Since he came to lead us, since he took our hand.
Sheep and cattle are fattening on the tall sweet grass,
Since he's been elected, all this has come to pass.

The economy is rising at an even rate,
His aim is more employment in every state.
Who is this man, nicknamed so grand?
He might make this country into the promised land.
His name is Bob Hawke of the eagle eye,
He'll watch over us. He will do or die.

© 1984 Valerie Dawson

> N.B. When Bob Hawke came to office a terrible drought that had gripped many parts of Australia broke. His nickname was then 'The Messiah'.

A Tribute to Ron Grant

Ron Grant — Bakerman with zest,
When it comes to marathon running,
You can rise, you can rise, you can rise, above the rest.

He hails from up Caboolture way,
Which is near the Sunshine Coast,
A bread carter by profession,
Which is a job to toast.

When he got this thought to go a distance,
No other man had done,
He started in by training,
With a seven kilometre run.

In 1977 he made his first long distance run,
From Bundaberg to Caboolture,
His new idea of fun.
Two years later from Sydney to Brisbane,
He set the Aussie record straight,
By running up the Birdsville Track,
   and crossed the arid Simpson Waste.

During twelve long years he's run for more
Than twice around the world.
He's seen road, grass, trees, sky,
Before his eyes unfurl.

VALERIE DAWSON

In March '83 he set out,
From Brisbane's Queen Street Mall,
To try to be the first to do the long
Round Australia haul.
Sixty-two kilometres a day he ran,
Without a single break
Till in October '83, he finally got back to his state.

Oh! What a superhuman achievement,
The agony you felt could not be vent.
Oh! What a tremendous psychological feat,
Whatever the cost – you would not know defeat.
So we took our hats off to you Ron,
And gave you a mighty cheer.
Then for your great marathon running,
We made you "Queenslander of the Year".

Now the Irishman Rafferty challenged you
To a last gruelling run,
'Twas a four-day race in searing, scorching heat,
The world's first summer desert one.
In fifty degree heat you set out,
Along a three eighty kilometre trail,
You ran, you staggered, you sweated, you walked,
But never once did you fail.

Over a thousand spinifexed sand dunes,
You ambled along in low gear.
At the Birdsville Pub they celebrated your win,
With an icy cold drink of beer.

We took our hats off once more Ron,
You're our bakerman with zest.
When it comes to marathon running,
You can rise, you can rise, you can rise, above the rest.

VALERIE DAWSON

Places Close to my Heart: Queensland

Icon vector created by rawpixel.com/freepik.com

Valerie Dawson

Bountiful Queensland

Queensland, most Bountiful Queensland,
With your climate so great,
What a glorious fate,
Just to live in this State.
To be part of this State.

Verse 1

First settlement was Humpy Bong on beautiful Moreton Bay.
Then free men came when Cunningham's Gap opened up the way
To grow sheep and wheat on the Darling Downs was their only goal,
Later on at Ipswich, Welsh helped to mine for coal.

Verse 2

When Gympie's gold rush saved you from going broke or worse.
For the first time in your history, you had money in your purse.
Then you started prospering, when you revealed all your resources,
Tin, copper, silver, lead, and zinc, now we spoke in many voices.

Verse 3

As vast tracts of land were opened up, and called "our Selections"
Farmers grew cattle, crops and cane, and lived in slab erections.

Your brave young men marched off to fight in many cruel wars.
Members of Parliament were elected, to legislate just laws.

Verse 4
Fine cities grew from country towns all along your coast,
To tourists from around the world, you became the perfect host,
As they toured the Barrier Reef, beaches and your scenic sights.
How hard you've strived and achieved, now your future looks bright.

(c) 2006.

Most Bountiful Queensland (No. 1)

Queensland, most Bountiful Queensland,
With its climate so great,
What a glorious fate
Just to be in this State.
So be part of it mate
Yes! Be part of it mate.

Come now, on a visit to Queensland,
Don't hesitate, just make a date,
With Australia's Sun State,
See this wonderful place.
This most bountiful State
This most bountiful State.

(c) 2009 V. Dawson. CD made from poem.

Valerie Dawson

Most Bountiful Queensland (no. 2)

Queensland, most Bountiful Queensland,
With its climate so great,
What a glorious fate
Just to be in this State.
So be part of it mate,
Yes! Be part of it mate.

Come now, come and visit the Gold Coast
Come here and toast,
The place with the most.
Book a great Gold Coast date,
in Australia's Sun State.
See this wonderful place,
This most bountiful State.

(c) 2009 V. Dawson.

Brisbane: My Favourite Place

Brisbane City's my favourite place,
A beaut city, with charm and a city of grace
Highest building was the iconic Town Hall,
Now they rise everywhere so stately and tall,
And where the steel lines were installed,
There's now the trendy Queen Street Mall.

Jacaranda and Poinciana trees flowering in the parks,
City lights reflecting on the river when it's dark.
The people, the Ekka and South Bank,
Your bonza bridges and such.
All there is to like about Brissie,
I like very much.

Though I've known you since you were a child,
And now you're all grown up and styled.
You'll be my place forever
These two ties we'll not sever.

Your Mount Coot-tha, with great views that go on forever,
And your wonderful, wending, winding Brisbane River.

© 2011 Music & Vocals V. Dawson
Played by D. Cobbin.
YouTube: http://bit.ly/BrisbaneSong

Valerie Dawson

Heritage Ipswich City

Heritage Ipswich city,
Is a great place to live.
Ipswich is the city,
With so much to offer and give.

There's affordable housing
And excellent schools,
Good public transport, and
Clean swimming pools.

Fine Hospitals, Libraries,
Art Gallery and more,
And quaint shops and buildings
For you to explore.

At Queen's Park, near the centre of town
An animal sanctuary can be found.
There are glorious views from the old-fashioned look-out,
And a playground where children can frolic and shout.
While all around, entertainment venues abound.
Shoppers up here are well catered for,
With Riverlink, Booval, Redbank and more.

So come on a visit to this friendly place.
You'll feel so at ease, have a smile on your face.
In which city? Ipswich city,
The city where you'll like to be.
So come on a visit and see.

© 2008 By V. & J. Dawson. Made CD. Played by D. Cobbin

IPSWICH. THE HERITAGE CITY

This heritage city of Queensland,
Is a great place to live.
This pioneering city of Queensland,
Has much to offer and give.
Our indigenous people have called this place home.
For millennia here, they would gather, hunt, and roam.

Coal mining was the first source of wealth for the town.
Then factories, mills and foundries
Sprang up all around.

The oldest school in the state was
The Ipswich Grammar,
And the lifeblood of the town was
The River Bremer.

There was a plan to make Ipswich the capital city,
But Brisbane won out—
Oh! What a pity.

With historic churches, houses and buildings.
And a hospital second to none...
An art gallery, library, rail museum,
And venues where people have fun.

Nearby is the main R.A.A.F. Base in the land,
Where Globemasters rule, so mighty and grand.
There's Willowbank Raceway and Bundamba Racetrack,
Where each year for The Cup, the punters come back.

VALERIE DAWSON

At Queen's Park, near the centre of town,
An animal sanctuary can be found.
With glorious views from the old-fashioned look-out,
And a playground where children can frolic and shout.

It's a city that welcomes both young and old.
Where babies are born in numbers untold.
The mayor is showing the old town in a new light.
Oh! Ipswich, Ipswich, your future looks bright.

© 2006 By V. and J. Dawson

ODE TO BRISBANE

Brisbane, oh Brisbane, my wonderful place,
Queensland's capital of charm and of grace,
Once there was just the iconic City Hall,
Now skyscrapers rise so stately and tall,
And where tram lines once were,
There's now the Queen Street Mall.

Though I've known you since you were a child,
And now you're all grown up and styled.
Still, I'll love you forever,
These ties we'll not sever,
Mount Coot-Tha, the Story Bridge,
And your winding, wending Brisbane River.

(c) 2009 V. Dawson

Valerie Dawson

Sydney on the Harbour

Sydney City, the harbour City,
Sydney City so chic and pretty.
Built on such a fabulous spot,
Tourists from 'round the world all flock.

Many years ago you were Sydney Town,
When Captain Phillip landed on your ground,
And convicts worked hard all year round,
Creating Sydney on the Harbour.

There's Hyde Park and Mrs. Macquarie's Chair,
With glorious gardens on show everywhere.
Taronga Park Zoo for a Ferryboat fare,
At beautiful Sydney on the Harbour.

See the Opera House so great and grand,
Built for opera lovers and concert fans.
Visit Bondi Beach for a surf and a tan,
At amazing Sydney on the Harbour.

Known as "The Coat Hanger"
There's a gigantic span,
And Luna Park, with its big laughing man.
Ships and yachts on the water, and catamarans,
At sparkling Sydney on the Harbour.

© 2014 Valerie Dawson

REDCLIFFE BY THE SEA

From the red cliffs of Redcliffe Peninsula,
One can gaze out across Moreton Bay.
These wonderful red cliffs of Redcliffe.
Flinders espied and named them one day.

On a clear day Moreton Island can be viewed,
And even some of Bribie as well,
Ships anchored, waiting to go to the Port.
Fishing dinghies if there's not too much swell.

Yachts on their way racing to Gladstone,
At Easter, what a sight to behold!
Go casually strolling 'long the foreshore,
Or have a swim if the day's not too cold.

A spot of fishing from the long Jetty,
Sounds to me like a bonza idea.
Or dine at an open-air cafe,
Where someone you know might appear.

From a boat why not do some whale watching,
Or see pelicans dive after fish.
Children happily playing on beaches,
Join in the fun and games if you wish.

On a bright Sunday come browse at the Markets,
Where a variety of goods are on show.

VALERIE DAWSON

There's produce, handcrafts, clothing and more,
If you see for yourself, then you'll know.

When visiting the Redcliffe Peninsula,
You're guaranteed to have such a great time.
The people are friendly, the place popular,
And it has the most marvellous clime.

© 2014 Valerie Dawson

The Mighty Mares

Image: Clipart.email

Valerie Dawson

Our Star – Black Caviar

There's a horse in Australia called 'Black Caviar'
Everyone knows of this great racing star.
She's a classy little mare
   with a good temperament
And her proud owners think
   she's been heaven sent.

Her racing colours are salmon
   with dots of black,
And her fans dress the same
   when they visit the track
They don't have a bet
   cause the odds are too low,
They just want to cheer her
   and see how she'll go.

She went to race at Ascot for the Queen's Jubilee.
They took her over there
So the whole world could see.
French horses nearly catching her—
But she had some to spare,
This wonderful, marvellous, gallant
Aussie Mare.

She's won all these races,
A five-year-old in all her glory,
Now, for twenty-five straight wins,
She'll go down in his-tory.

The Queen of the racing world
   is Black Caviar
Our great Aussie racehorse,
This mare is a star.

Valerie Dawson

One-in-a-Million Winx

There's a new kid on the block
With the name of Winx
A brilliant, talented racehourse
Every-one thinks.

Trainers from all over
Wanted this horse so plucky
But unfortunately for them
They didn't get that lucky.

One owner, Peter Tighe
Chose a trainer, Chris Waller
Though the others found this
A bit hard to swallow.

Crowds flock to the courses
Hoping to catch a glimpse
Of this speedy, marvellous
One in a million Winx.

Most horses have four gears,
But she must have five
And this is what gives her
That extra bit of drive.

The ladies are excited
Some in blue frocks and hats

The chaps don't put a bet on
'Cause the odds are so flat

They all cheer, clap, and jump around
Whenever Winx races
But she never gets startled,
And just goes through her paces.

A third Cox Plate she won
Our favourite Winx,
And she finished almost faster than
Our eyes could blink.

Will she beat Black Caviar's record
Of twenty-five in a row?
We wish you luck, you little beauty
So go girl, go!!

© 2018 Valerie Dawson
Two poems now in Hall of Fame, Racing Museum, Flemington, Vic.

VALERIE DAWSON

Valerie Dawson

The Sydney Olympics are Here

The Sydney Olympics are here at last,
And the waiting game is over and past.
For this great show we have a wonderful cast
The Sydney Olympics are here.

The athletes have trained hard, they'll all give their best,
Swimmers, runners, and gymnasts—and
All of the rest.
The city is crowded with tourists galore,
Excited by all that the games have in store.

The stadium's ready and all the venues,
Restaurants are serving exotic menus.
The harbour's all decked out in fine fancy dress,
'Cause all of the world we are keen to impress.

So shout hip-hooray and then all give a cheer,
After all, it's the greatest event of the year.
It's the Sydney Olympics, the Sydney Olympics,
The Sydney Olympics are here.

© 2000 Music and vocals: V. Dawson
Played by: D. Cobbin
YouTube: http://bit.ly/Syd2000song

This poem was made into a CD and video. Opened the Roy & H.G. show on Channel 7 on a Saturday night. Valerie was awarded a golden wombat. Also played on Sunrise for 2 weeks.

Gold Coast Commonwealth Games are Here

Gold Coast Commonwealth Games are here at last,
And the waiting time is over and past,
For this great Show we have a wonderful cast,
Gold Coast Commonwealth Games are here.

The Athletes have trained hard, they'll all give their best,
Swimmers, Runners, and Gymnasts and all of the rest.
The Gold Coast is crowded, with Tourists galore,
Excited by all that the Games have in store.

The Stadium's ready and all the Venues,
Restaurants are serving exotic Menus.
The Beaches are decked out in fine fancy dress,
'Cause all of the world we are keen to impress.

So shout "hip-hooray" and let's all give a cheer,
After all, it's the greatest event of the year,
It's the Gold Coast Commonwealth Games,
The Gold Coast Commonwealth Games,
Gold Coast Commonwealth Games are here.

© 2016 Valerie Dawson
Adapted from 'The Sydney Olympics are Here'

Valerie Dawson

ODE TO THE BRONCOS

Let's hear it for the B–R–O–N–C–O–S
The best footy team in the land
Our brave steeds, Brisbane Broncos,
We all think you're just grand.

With your brilliant passes, tackles and scrums,
And when you score those goals,
You are our favourite sons.
We've come to see you and cheer you along,
And while we're here we'll all join in,
This rousing Bronco song

'Cause you're the best footy team,
The maroon footy team,
The greatest league team in the land,
No wonder we think you're so grand.
Yes! You're the B–R–O–N–C–O–S
B–R–O–N–C–O–S
Yeah!
The B–R–O–N–C–O–S

© 2007. CD made.
Music and vocals: V. Dawson
Played by: D. Cobbin

ODE TO THE MAROONS

Let's hear it for M A R O O N S, [SPELL IT]

The best footy team in the land.
Our brave players for Queensland,
We all think you're just grand.

With your brilliant passes, tackles and scrums,
And when you score those tries
   you're all our favourite sons.
We've come to see you, and cheer you along,
And while we're here, we'll all join in this rousing, loyal song.

'Cause you're the best footy team,
The Maroon footy team,
The greatest league team in the land.
No wonder we think you're so grand.
Yes! you're the M A R OO N, M A R OO N [SPELL IT]
M A R OO N S, YEAH!!
The Maroons.

© 2012. Adapted from "Ode to the Broncos"
Music and vocals V. Dawson
Played by D. Cobbin

ODE TO THE WEST COAST EAGLES

The West Coast Eagles
They soar through the air.
They will do or dare.

The West Coast Eagles
Have a fabulous name.
They play a just – and fair – game.
No wonder they've earned
Such far-reaching fame.

The great West Coast Eagles
Have soared and scored.

© 2018 Valerie Dawson

Poems for Children

Valerie Dawson

Welcome K.C. the Cat

I have a little bundle of fur,
It's name is K.C. the cat.
Although it's supposed to be a boy,
I'm not too sure of that.

But whatever it turns out to be,
This cat that's black and white,
I'll feed and look after it,
And let it sleep with me at night.

I'll welcome it into my home and heart,
'Cause it will bring me joy.
This cute and playful ball of fluff,
Be it a girl or a boy.

(c) 2015 Valerie Dawson

In Memory of Laleh

Laleh was such a special kind of cat.
No one could doubt the truth of that.
From a tiny kitten Jane did rear her,
Fed, loved her, and brushed her fur.

She also liked salmon from a can,
But above all else she was Val's greatest fan.
Whenever she heard her CDs play,
She would come a running to listen and stay.

She enjoyed climbing up trees and the roof,
And sometimes she appeared a little aloof.
Hunting birds and mice was her great skill,
And chasing 'possums gave her a thrill.

Her favourite thing was to snuggle on a lap,
And she only liked water from the tank tap.
She loved to sleep in cupboards among the clothes,
But was really scared of the garden hose.

Laleh would wake Don before the sun was up,
Sit with him in the kitchen while he had his cup.
Then both off to the verandah bed in the sun
Lazing around when there was work to be done!

Valerie Dawson

We will miss little Laleh very much we fear,
But to Jane she was the pet she held most dear.

© 2015 Valerie Dawson

Happy Australia Day

Australia Day, Australia Day,
We all love Australia Day.
The animals and birds love it too,
And this is what they all do...

The Kookaburra laughs, the Koala growls,
The Magpie warbles a tune,
The Wombat digs, the Kangaroo jumps,
While the Dingo waits for the moon.

The Bandicoot burrows, the Cockatoo squawks,
The Crocodile basks in the sun.
The Pelican fishes, the tree snake hisses,
While the Galah just likes to have fun.

The Goanna runs fast, the Platypus swims,
The Bilby hops along,
While the Emu scratches with its claw,
They all join in a song.

Soon the barbecue is ready,
With a feast fit for a king.
Then afterwards they all play games,
Gathered round in a ring.

Oh! What a lovely happy way,
To celebrate Australia Day,

VALERIE DAWSON

Australia Day, Australia Day
Our great Australia Day.

(c) 2008 Val Dawson. Made into CD.
Music & vocals V. Dawson, Played D. Cobbin

Making Easter Eggs

The happy Easter Bunnies come hopping along,
Hop, hop, hopping along.

The chirpy Easter chickens come chirping along,
Chirp, chirp, chirping their song.

The quacky Easter ducks come quacking along,
Waddling in the sun
While the long-eared Bilbies join in the fun.

Then they all gather round in a ring,
To enjoy a little dance and all together sing.

Later they get busy making eggs and shapes to store,
To give on Easter Day to every girl and boy.

Yes! The happy Easter bunnies come visiting,
On Easter Day each year,
Bringing lots of goodies... and Easter cheer
So be sure to leave a carrot out,
When Easter time is near.

© 2008 Valerie Dawson. Put to the music of "The Easter Song".

Valerie Dawson

The Xmas Bilbies

Now Xmas time will soon be around,
So the bilbies start to come out of the ground,
Santa Claus is going to need a little help,
For he, Mrs Claus and his cute little elves.

Long-eared bilbies love Xmas so much,
That they write to Santa Claus and keep in touch.
They are flying to the North Pole all rugged up,
But they'll have to cover up their ears with fluff.

Santa Claus is pleased they've come to help,
Jumps up and down for joy, and so do the elves.
They make video games, cars, trains, and building blocks,
Cute cuddly animals, pretty dolls and frocks.

Now Santa has lots and lots of toys
To bring on his sleigh to all the girls and boys,
Yes, the cute long-eared bilbies love Xmas time,
With Xmas trees all tinselled and fairy lights that shine.

(c) 2010 Valerie Dawson
Adapted for a CD.

YOU'RE NEVER TOO OLD FOR SANTA CLAUS

by Jane Dawson

You're never too old for Santa Claus,
You're never too old to have fun.
You're never too old for Santa Claus,
The jolly white bearded one.
So go get a photo with Santa Claus,
You'll be glad you got it done.

You're never too old for Santa Claus,
Or too big to sit on his knee.
You're never too old for Santa Claus,
'Cause Santa loves you and me.
So go make a wish with Santa Claus,
Underneath the Xmas tree.

You're never too old for Santa Claus,
His story will always be told.
You're never too old for Santa Claus,
'Cause Santa's got a heart of gold.
So go write a letter to Santa Claus,
And address it to the North Pole.

You're never too old for Santa Claus,
You're never too old to believe.
You're never too old for Santa Claus,
He's a friend that we all need.
So have a little faith in Santa Claus,
Then there's nothing he can't achieve.

(c) 2010 Jane Dawson. Made into CD.

www.ingramcontent.com/pod-product-compliance
Lightning Source LLC
Chambersburg PA
CBHW070440010526
44118CB00014B/2128